D.McDonald Designs Sunflowers & Sayings Adult Coloring Book

Welcome
Get out all
your colors and have fun!
Be sure to place
paper behind the
page you are working on
to protect the next page!
This book includes
a bonus section
of images perfect
for framing along
with the full size images.

D.McDonald Designs Sunflowers & Sayings Adult Coloring Book

It is about
You

But Not All
about You !

Be
Bright
Be
A
Happy
Sight !

D. McDonald Designs

SunFlowers
&
Sayings

Adult Coloring Book

Colored By:

Cleo Fraser

D. McDonald Designs
Sunflowers & Sayings
Adult Coloring Book

There is Always Something to Smile About

Life is
filled with
MAGIC

It Doesn't
Matter
If
The Glass Is
Half Full
OR
Half Empty

Just be
Happy
You Have
A Glass !

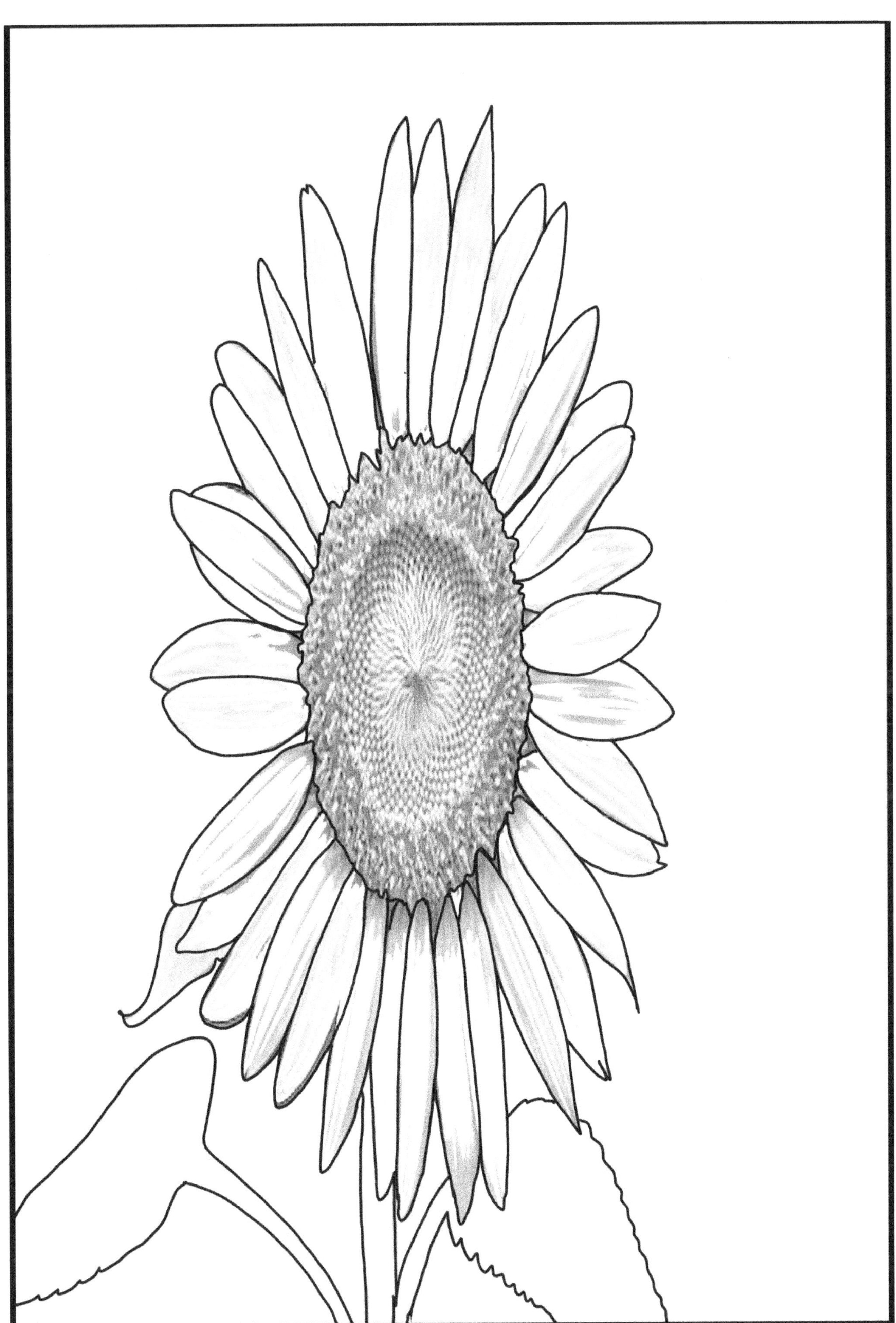

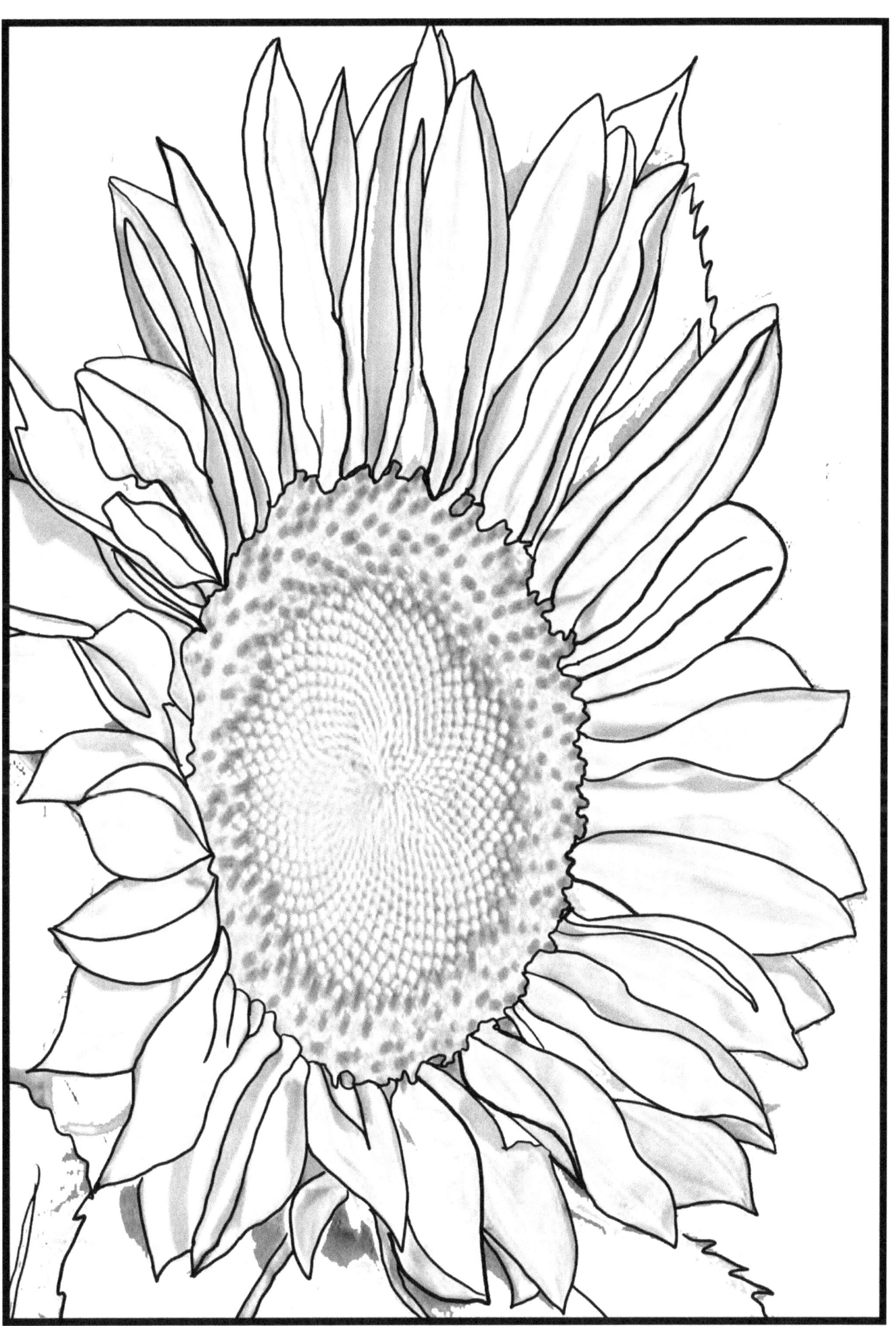

It is about You

But Not All about You !

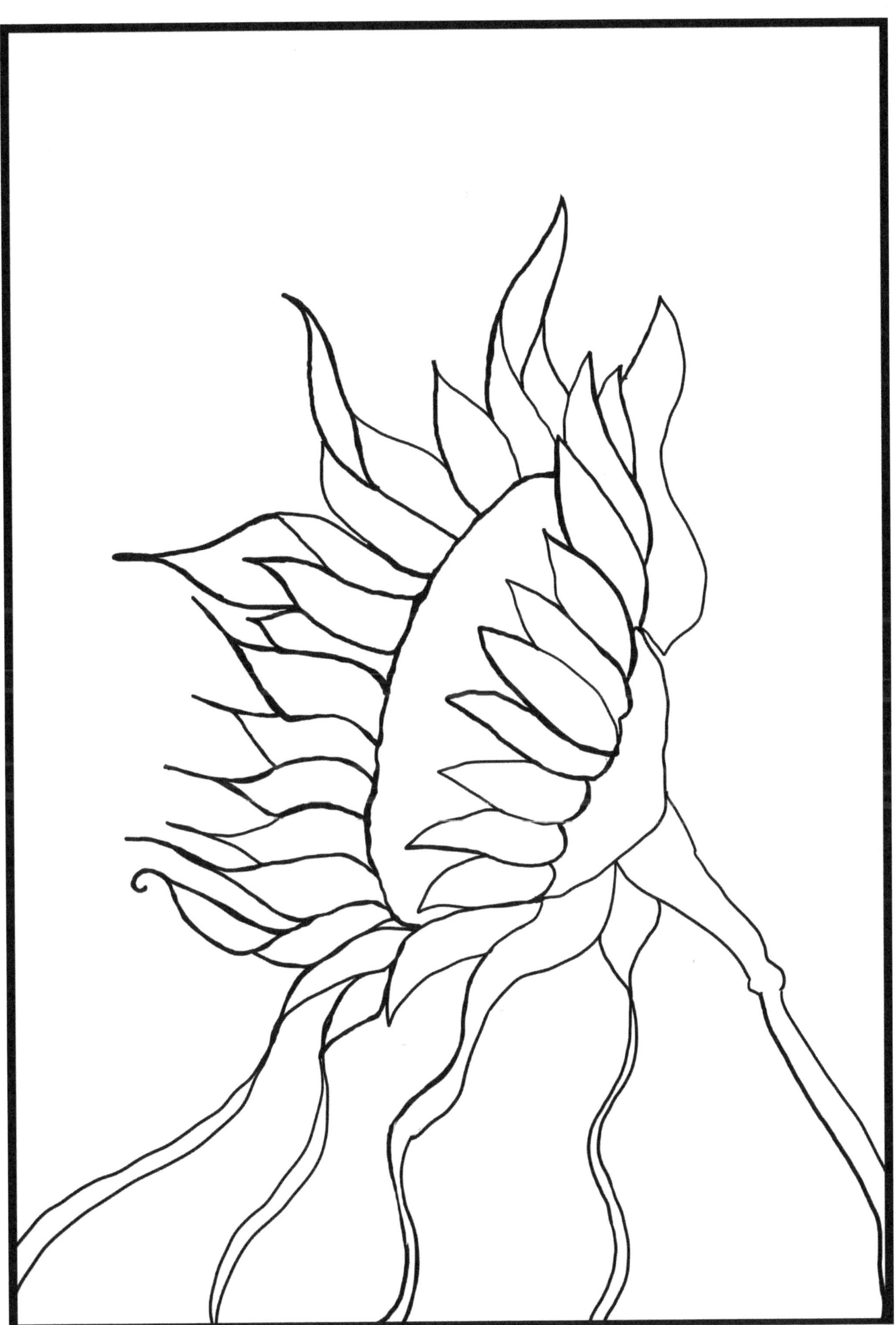

Be
Bright
Be
A
Happy
Sight!

I
AM
the
Sunshine

I
AM
the
SUNShine

Smile

Smile

MAY YOUR Blessings Out number Your Sheep!

There is Always Something to Smile About

There is Always Something to Smile About

It Doesn't
Matter
If
The Glass Is
Half Full
OR
Half Empty

Just be
Happy
You Have
A Glass !

It is about
You

But Not All
about You !

Be
Bright
Be
A
Happy
Sight!

D. McDonald Designs
Sunflowers & Sayings
Adult Coloring Book

D. McDonald Designs
Sunflowers & Sayings
Adult Coloring Book

It Doesn't
Matter
If
The Glass Is
Half Full
OR
Half Empty

Just be
Happy
You Have
A Glass !

D. McDonald Designs
Sunflowers & Sayings
Adult Coloring Book

D. McDonald Designs
Sunflowers & Sayings
Adult Coloring Book

D. McDonald Designs
Sunflowers & Sayings
Adult Coloring Book

D. McDonald Designs
Sunflowers & Sayings
Adult Coloring Book

D. McDonald Designs
Sunflowers & Sayings
Adult Coloring Book

D. McDonald Designs
Good Witch, Bad Witch, Sandwich
Coloring Book

D.McDonald Designs

Halloween Coloring Book 2018

D. McDonald Designs
Welcome To My Garden Coloring Book

d. mcdonald designs

{5} Fabulous Florals Two

D.McDonald Designs

Home Tweet Home Adult Coloring Book

D.McDonald Designs

Mandala Adult Coloring Book 2018

D.McDonald Designs
Christmas Coloring Book 2018

D.McDonald Designs
Christmas Coloring Book 2018

D.McDonald Designs
Christmas Coloring Book 2018

D. McDonald Designs
The Complete Gray Scale Stained Glass Collection
Adult Coloring Book

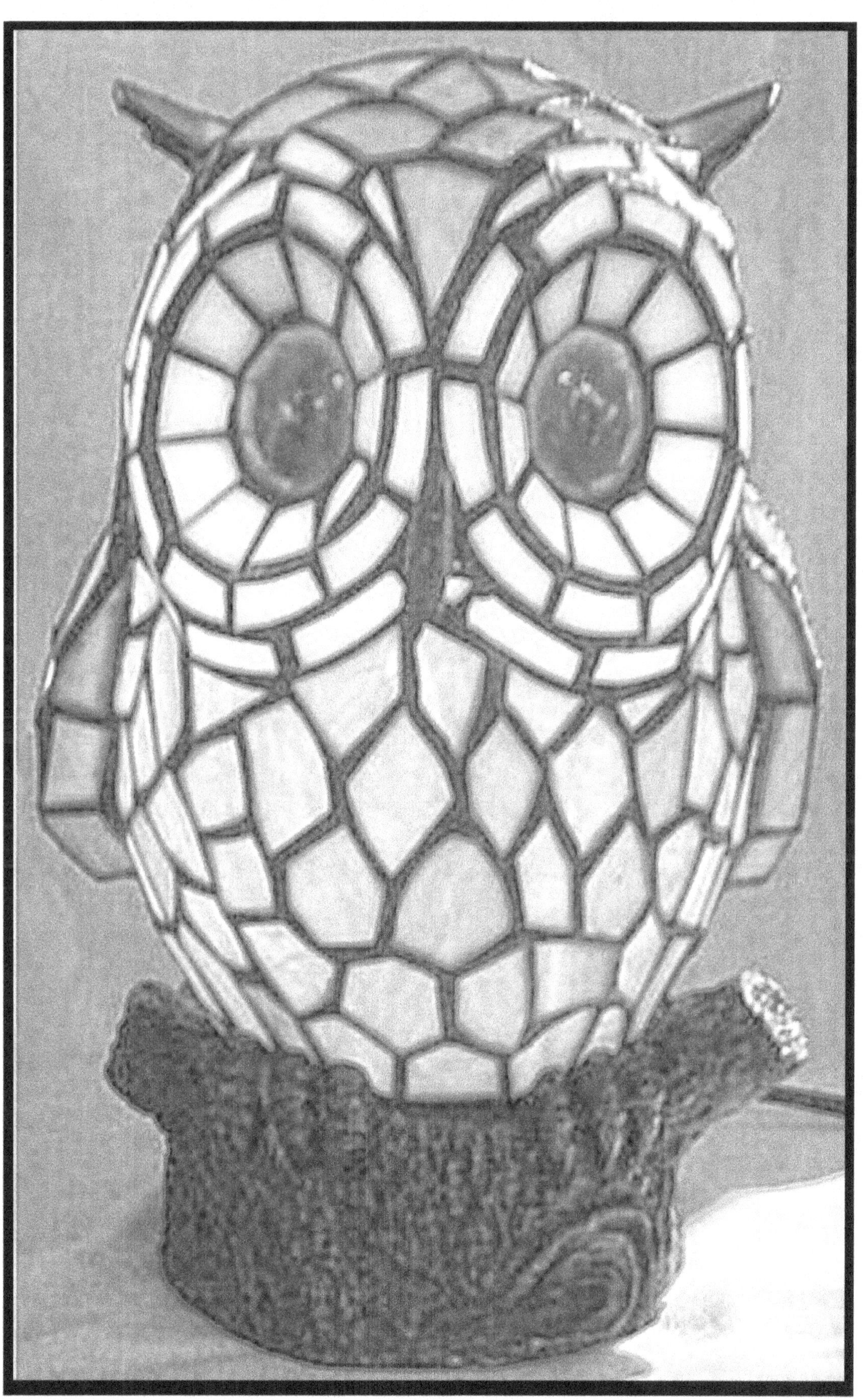

D.McDonald Designs

Halloween Coloring Book 2018